Fun Walks
Devon
Axminster

Paul & Heather Hampton

For our dear friend Jane who gave up her time to proofread our Fun Walks series of books, and for her very special dog Guinness.

ISBN: 9781723951749

CONTENTS

A view to Axminster from Trinity Hill

INTRODUCTION

Welcome.

The Tourist Information Centre (TIC) is based in the Heritage Museum in Axminster and Heather has volunteered there from time to time. She has often been asked if there are any local walks and whether there are any fun things to do in Axminster. This gave us the idea of writing a series of books combining local walks with optional games to keep everyone amused along the way.

Visit the website www.funwalks.co.uk for information on other books in the Fun Walks series.

We are of the opinion that no matter how old you are, you can still be young at heart. This book is therefore for everyone who enjoys getting out and about for a walk and having fun!

There are many places of interest to visit in the Axe Valley and East Devon; we have only suggested a few which you will find on pages 37 and 38. If you would like more information on things to do in this area, why not pay a visit to the TIC and the Heritage Museum where friendly volunteers will be more than happy to help.

Paul & Heather Hampton

"You're never too old to have fun!"

HOW TO USE THIS BOOK

Heritage Centre and TIC

Many of the walks start from the Heritage Centre Museum in Axminster with a couple starting on the outskirts of town. All walks have a brief summary giving the length, types of surface and key features of the walk.

There is an Ordnance Survey map for each walk clearly marked with numbers to help you navigate. Just follow the walks starting at number ❶. Recommended parking for each walk is also given and indicated by a 🅿 symbol on the map.

For those travelling by foot, First Bus operate bus services that cover this and other Fun Walks books in the local South West region. Please see the company's website for bus timetables and an online route planner: www.firstgroup.com/wessex-dorset-south-somerset

We suggest appropriate footwear should be worn as some parts of the walks can be muddy in wet weather. Some of the walks are on country lanes and roads so although traffic will be light on most, please take care. Distances are provided to help you navigate the routes but note they are all approximate.

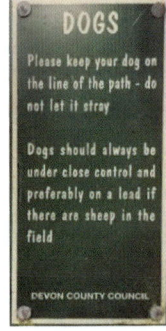

At the time of writing, all walks are dog friendly but please respect any local signage you encounter, especially around children's playgrounds, and keep your dog on a lead in fields where there are livestock.

All walks were verified at the time of publication but visit the Fun Walks website (www.funwalks.co.uk) to check for updates.

Walking in the lovely Axe Valley is pleasurable in itself, but to add some fun, the walks include optional puzzles as described on the next page. Other games to play on the way can be found at the back of the book, along with suggestions for refreshment stops and places of interest you may wish to visit.

PUZZLES

There are different puzzles to solve along each of the walks.

Observation Challenges are indicated by a spy glass; simply answer the question posed.

Spot The Picture puzzles are indicated by a pinned Polaroid picture – see if you can find the scene or object on your walk.

WP **Word Puzzles** give you clues to letters that form an anagram. Rearrange all the letters you have found on the walk to solve the puzzle. Some of the letters are also numbered; copy the numbered letter to the corresponding space or spaces in the grid that you will find on page 34. This will then form a final sentence that will be revealed when all the walks are completed.

For those completing the **Observation Challenges** and **Word Puzzles** in the book, there will be a downloadable personalised certificate available from the website www.funwalks.co.uk

Gold, Silver or Bronze certificates will be awarded, depending on the number of walks completed with correct answers. Good Luck!

Visit the website for more information and to submit your answers.

If you would prefer not to write your answers in the book, there is a downloadable questionnaire sheet available on the website to print before you start the walk.

Why not become part of the **Fun Walks** family by entering our annual **prize photography competition** or owning a **Fun Walks badge!** Please see the website and online shop for details.

WALK 1 – TOWN AND RIVER

View from the river Axe across the Axe Valley

This is a circular 2 mile walk around parts of the town and the river Axe. The route starts in the town and then leads you down by the river with views over the Axe Valley. The walk is mostly level on pavements and some footpaths cross farm fields. There is one unmanned level crossing to be aware of, please take care as you cross. There are several opportunities for refreshments in the town, some are listed on pages 37 and 38.

Parking: Coombe Lane Car Park, Coombefield Lane, EX13 5AX

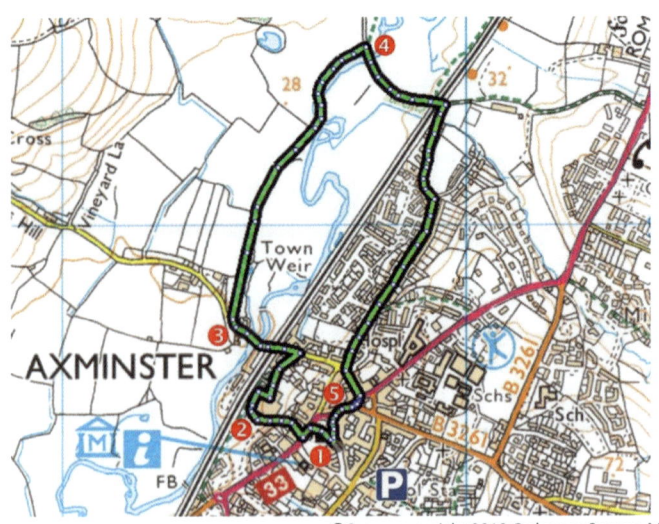

©Crown copyright 2019 Ordnance Survey. Media 052/19

❶ Start at the Heritage Centre which is in Silver Street (EX13 5AH). With the Centre on your right, head towards the church of St Mary's. Walk around the church to **Spot The Picture**.

If you have time, pop into St Mary's church, the oldest building in the town with much of the structure dating from the 13th-15th centuries. The church is almost certainly the only one in the country laid with Axminster carpet. In 1755, Thomas Whitty commenced weaving on the first carpet to be made in Axminster. Subsequently, when a new

carpet was finished, it was often carried through the streets of the town to the sound of the bells from the church of St. Mary's. Continue the walk by exploring the church green where you will find several seats.

WP *One of the seats on the church green commemorates a queen. What is the first letter of her name?* _____

To continue the walk, go down the steps that are in between the greens to the main high street and turn left to the pedestrian crossing. Use this to cross over to the Post Office and turn right. After a few yards turn left through a metal arch with the words "Belle Vue Access to Tesco" above. Follow the path and you will come across a sculpture of a farmer with his cow and the Sublyme café on your left. You will now head down to Tesco supermarket either using the steps or ramps. On your way down you will find another **Spot The Picture.**

❷ At the bottom of the ramp, use the pedestrian crossing and make your way to the front of the store using the pavement. At the front of the store, head left towards the trees past the ATM machines and turn right onto a path at the corner of the building.

Follow this path to emerge onto an access road and maintain direction to the next road junction opposite the Jaffé Feather Factory. Turn left and continue carefully across the level crossing. Keep a look out for trains and cross the bridge passing over the river Axe.

 Find a plaque and take the 1st letter from the name of the event the defence scheme protects against. _____

A few yards after the bridge you will see a gate into a field on your right next to a house.

3 Go through the gate into this field and follow the path to go through a kissing gate. Maintain direction to a gate and

pass into another field. Follow the field edge to another kissing gate and continue, keeping the river and trees close to your right. After a further kissing gate, the river and path bend to the left then right; follow the well-defined path next to the river aiming for the bridge ahead. At another kissing gate go up the steps to a road.

4 Turn right when you emerge onto the road and cross the bridge. Look around, there is a **Spot The Picture.**

 Find the private fishing sign and take the 2nd letter from the Somerset town whose club is allowed to fish here. _____

Continue up the road and after 200 yards cross a bridge over the railway line and take the first right down a lane.

Keep to this lane as it bends to the left then immediately right. After about 300 yards you will pass a children's playground on your right. Continue to the end of the road and turn left up the hill past the Castle Inn pub. When you come to a fork in the road in front of a large building (The George Hotel), bear right, crossing the junction carefully and keep to the right hand side of the pavement as the road bends round past Costa Coffee. Along this pavement you can **Spot The Picture.**

Near here is a plaque commemorating a famous journey made by horse and carriage in 1805. How many times did the rider change horses on the trip? _____

 Take the 4th letter from the name of the Cape where the famous sea battle took place. _____

5 Continue along the pavement and in a few yards, cross the road using the pedestrian crossing opposite River Cottage Canteen and Deli and turn right. You will now find yourself in Trinity Square with its distinctive Victorian fountain. A market is held in the square every Thursday morning.

 The fountain commemorates a milestone in Queen Victoria's reign – take the 1st letter from the name of this anniversary. _____

Keep to the left hand side of the square and take the road that veers left until you reach the Heritage Centre. The Centre is worth visiting if you haven't already done so.

 Rearrange the 5 **Word Puzzle** letters you have found and make a word. You may have spotted this name on your walk.

— — — — —
15   13

WALK 2 – LYME ROAD AND FAIRACRE

View to Axminster from Fairacre

This is a circular 2 mile walk that starts in the town but soon takes you uphill and across fields with excellent views back to Axminster and the surrounding countryside. The walk also passes through a well-equipped playground that might be of interest if you have younger companions.

Parking: Coombe Lane Car Park, Coombefield Lane, EX13 5AX

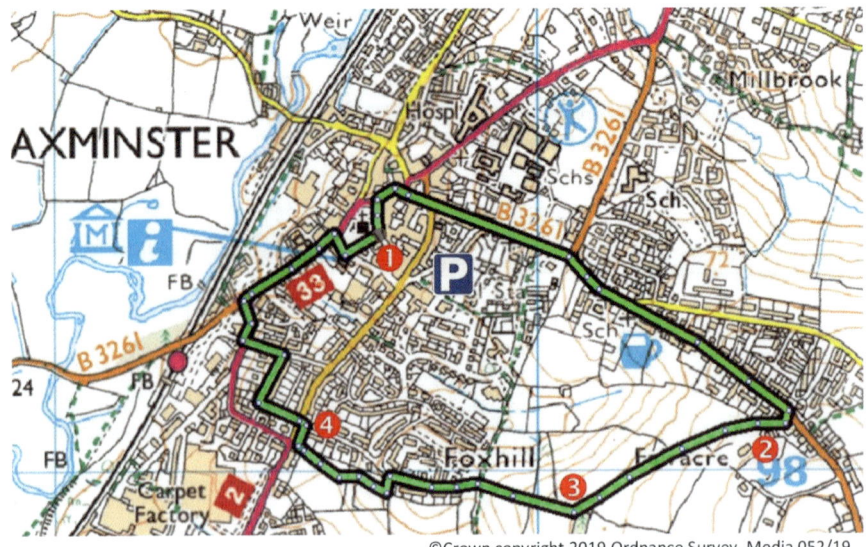

©Crown copyright 2019 Ordnance Survey. Media 052/19

❶ Start at the Heritage Centre which is in Silver Street (EX13 5AH). With the Centre on your right, follow the road to the town square, keeping to the pavement on the right. Pass River Cottage Canteen and Deli and continue on this side of the road as it slowly bends round along Trinity Square. Pass the NCP Car Park on your right and at the junction cross over carefully and maintain direction up the road, which now becomes Lyme Road.

After about 200 yards you will see the entrance to the Axminster Leisure Centre and Swimming Pool on your left. Carefully cross here to **Spot The Picture**.

W P *The swimming pool is named after a bird; take the 3rd last letter of the name of this bird.* _____

Maintain direction up the hill staying on the left hand side of the road. Ignore the turning to Stoney Lane and Sector Lane and keep straight ahead on Lyme Road. You will eventually see a pub across the road on your right.

W P *The pub is named after a farm animal; take the 2nd letter of the animal's name.* _____

The pub is 19th century; in which year was it built? _____

Continue up the hill to pass a petrol station on the other side of the road. In a further few hundred yards, look for a lane on the other side of the road by Cowslip House and cross the road carefully to take this lane. Here there is another **Spot The Picture.**

❷ After a few yards, go through a gate into the field that appears on the right by the entrance to Fairacre.

Once in the field, continue on the path that is fairly well marked along the top of the hill. The area will open up and you will soon see good views down to the town and beyond. Stay on this path as it briefly passes through trees into the next field.

❸ At the end of this field you will emerge into another field but here you turn right downhill keeping the hedge to your right. At the bottom of the hill you arrive at a junction of finger posts; continue straight onto a road by houses. After 50 yards, take a turning left into Weller Road and take the next right into Swain Close. Keep to the road as it bends left and at the end, go through a gate into a recreation park with a fenced playground. Turn left down the slight incline and then head for the far righthand corner of the park.

Can you find a sea creature the likes of which would have lived millions of years ago? What is its name? _____

At the corner of the park you will find a path that takes you between houses to Boxfield Road.

WP *A yellow sign warns of two-way traffic on the road ahead. Take the 3rd letter of the name of the road on the sign.* _____

❹ Turn left and take the path on the opposite side of the intersecting road between two houses. At the end of the path turn right, and then at the end of the road turn left into Widepost Lane. Take care as there is no pavement on this lane. At the junction to a main road, turn right and head down to a roundabout. At the roundabout turn right heading back into town. Around here you can **Spot The Picture**.

This is one of the few remains of the JH Shand manufacturing business once located in this area.

Continue up the road to pass the entrance to the Co-op supermarket on your right.

W P *You will see a building on the other side of the road with a crest over the doorway. Take the middle letter from the second word in its name.* _____

Continue up the hill and take the first right into Church Street at the corner of Le Pisani's restaurant. After a few yards you will see the Arts Café and Bar on your right. The café is located next to a public garden in the former courthouse. The café is worth visiting to see the original prison cells now converted into dining areas. There is also some interesting art works either side of the entrance to the gardens.

Further along here is also the Archway Bookshop. The arched doorway to the shop is formed from stone taken from a now demolished Cistercian abbey dating from 1247.

W P *Read the blue plaque by the Archway Bookshop and find the 3rd last letter from the name of the abbey.* _____

Carefully cross the road to take the path almost directly opposite the bookshop. The path runs through a green to the right of the church and you will see further art work on the wall on your right. Turn right at the end of the path to return to the Heritage Centre where the walk began.

W P Rearrange the 5 **Word Puzzle** letters you have found to make a name from Axminster's past.

$$\overline{\underset{19}{\quad}}\ \overline{\underset{2}{\quad}}\ \overline{\quad}\ \overline{\underset{20}{\quad}}\ \overline{\underset{10}{\quad}}$$

WALK 3 – QUIET LANES AND COUNTRY VIEWS

View towards Smallridge

This is a 5 mile circular walk around the eastern side of Axminster. The initial part of the route will take you steadily uphill over fields and quiet lanes. It then levels off to enjoy good views back towards Axminster and the Axe Valley. The return journey heads downhill along a lane with further good views to the west. The final section takes you back into town along a cycle path.

Parking: Poplar Mount Car Park, 19 Poplar Mount. EX13 5QD

©Crown copyright 2019 Ordnance Survey. Media 052/19

1 Starting at the Poplar Mount Car Park, turn left into Chard Street and follow the pavement on the left hand side. Almost immediately you will encounter two historical buildings. The Church across the road on your right is where the founder of Axminster Carpets, Thomas Whitty is buried. You will also pass Oak House on your left, built in 1758, it was once described as the best house in Axminster. The house has served a number of purposes over the years and was at one time a school.

How many cherubs can you see on top of Oak House? _____

Continue on the road as it passes the hospital on your left and the entrance to Latches Walk will also soon appear on your left.

W P
— —
Take the 3rd last letter from the name of the gardens that Latches Walk leads to. _____

Continue straight ahead on Chard Street (now Chard Road) and head down the hill. When the pavement runs out at Millbrook Dale, cross carefully to the other side of the road and continue down to the mini roundabout. Cross using the traffic island on the right and look for a path only a few yards on your left between barriers; the entrance is marked by a blue shared footpath/cyclepath sign.

2 Follow the path as it bends right then left and takes you to a road. Keep straight ahead along this road for a few yards. When the road forks, look for a grassy path directly behind the road sign for Flax Meadow Lane. Follow this path with houses on your left and the stream on your right. The path will lead you back to a pavement next to houses. Go up two sets of steps and through a gate into a field. Follow the path that runs straight across the field to another gate. This gate is slightly to the right of where the finger post points so aim for the right of the farm buildings. You will now maintain direction and head downhill through two further field gates keeping the stream not far from sight on your right. After about ½ mile you will come to a road bridge that provides access to the Sector Park estate. Ignore this bridge but instead look for a small wooden footbridge only 30 yards further ahead. Cross this footbridge and in a few yards, go through a gate onto Sector Lane. Turn left up the road and take care as there is no pavement for the next ½ mile and you will encounter vehicles. After about ¼ mile you will see a turning to Coles Lane; here you can **Spot The Picture**.

❸ Continue for approximately ¼ mile along Sector Lane and then turn left into Cuthays Lane following it as it bends right. After 50 yards, ignore the track that appears next to a finger post on your left and keep right on the lane. You will soon start to see good views across the Axe Valley. After about 400 yards you will reach a finger post next to two farm gates. Keep right following the Public Bridleway sign. The track will soon bend round to the left and you will come to a well-defined track on your left next to a post with a blue way-marked arrow.

Follow the track through the field and at the end, go through the gate on your left into another field. Go straight across this field to a further gate. Ignore the finger-posted route on your left and go through the gate keeping right along the track with the field on your left. The track will lead you to Lodge Lane next to some buildings.

Opposite the track there is a building with some unusual metal chimney pots. How many pots does the building have? _____

W P
— —

Take the 1st letter from the name of the house on your right with a dragon in its name.   _____

4 Go left down Lodge Lane. There are no pavements and you may encounter the occasional vehicle so take care especially around bends. You will now follow this lane ignoring all footpath signs for 1½ miles. The lane makes its way downhill through a series of bends to Weycroft and Chard Road. Towards the end of the lane, buildings will appear on your right and you will come to Weycroft Manor. Here you can **Spot The Picture.**

Continue down the lane to reach Chard Road. Cross this very busy road with care and take the cycle path opposite signposted for Axminster.

 A brown sign at the start of the path points to a Weycroft building. Take the last two letters from the 2nd word.   _____

5 Go over the footbridge to follow the cycle path as it bends first right and then left. Continue on the path for ½ mile through 3 gates. After passing football pitches and a duck pond on your left, you will emerge onto a crossing track next to a skate park. Turn right here and then immediately left and follow this lane until it bends left.

 Here you will now see the name of the lane you are on. Take the 2nd and 5th letters from the name of this lane.   _____

Stay on the lane as it immediately turns right and continue on the road to a T-junction just beyond a children's playground. Go left up the hill past the Castle Inn pub and at the top opposite a large building (The George Hotel), turn left again. The Poplar Mount Car Park will be 100 yards up the hill on your left.

W P
— —   Rearrange the 6 **Word Puzzle** letters you have found to make a word. This was a feature of the early part of the walk.

$$\overline{}\quad\overline{}\quad\overline{}\quad\overline{}\quad\overline{}\quad\overline{}$$
11   7   21   3

15

WALK 4 – PUSHCHAIRS AND PLAYGROUNDS

View from Castle Hill

This is a short circular walk just over a mile in length suitable for families with young children and pushchairs. The walk takes in a small part of the town, some residential areas and visits 3 children's playgrounds. The route is mainly on tarmac apart from some of the entrances to the playgrounds; these are mainly grass or bark tracks but could be wet after rain.

Parking: Coombe Lane Car Park, Coombefield Lane, EX13 5AX

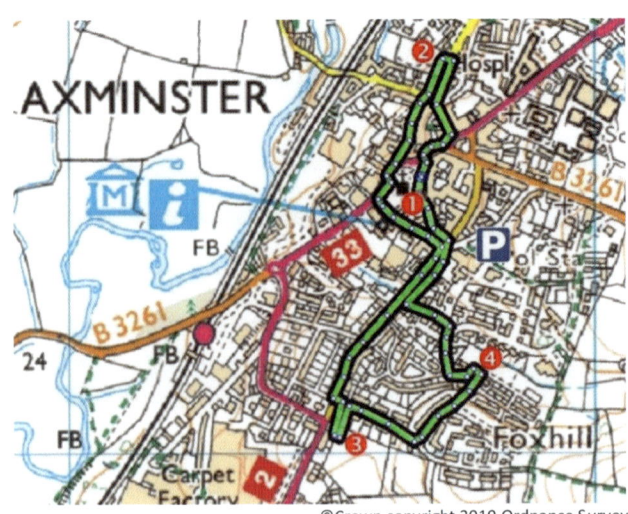

©Crown copyright 2019 Ordnance Survey. Media 052/19

❶ Start at the Heritage Centre which is in Silver Street (EX13 5AH). With the Centre on your right, follow the road to the square and keep to the pavement on the right. Pass some shops to reach the pedestrian crossing opposite River Cottage Canteen.

WP *River Cottage Canteen is a Kitchen and …. Take the 1ˢᵗ letter from the last word in its title.* _____

Go over the pedestrian crossing and turn right. Follow the pavement as it bends left past Costa Coffee and as the road forks, keep left downhill. After a few yards, look for a building on your left with a bell on its roof.

WP *Take the last letter from the last word of the building's original name.* _____

Now cross carefully to the other side of the road and continue downhill past a pub. Here you will be able to **Spot The Picture.**

WP *Take the 1ˢᵗ letter from the last word of the name of the pub.* _____

After a few further yards, take the first right into North Street and then after 50 yards or so, you will find your 1ˢᵗ playground.

❷ After you have visited the playground, continue your walk by retracing your steps along North Street to the main road. Now look for the road diagonally opposite on the right. Cross carefully and take this road to pass a garage on your right and The Old Chapel building on your left, which is now an antique and crafts centre. At the top of the road you will emerge onto the main street. Turn right and use the pedestrian crossing opposite the Post Office. Once across, turn right and keep to the left hand pavement as it bends left and continue along Church Street.

Across the road on your right you will see the Arts Café and Bar, which is adjacent to a public courtyard garden. The garden has easy access for a pushchair. The garden has a bandstand and there is often live music here on Saturdays in the summer. Continue along Church Street to pass a Medical Practice and a Care Home both located on the opposite side of the road.

WP   *Take the 1ˢᵗ letter from the name of the Care Home.*   _____

Take care here, as the pavement narrows for a few yards until you reach the corner of The Axminster Inn where Silver Street joins from the left. Cross the road carefully and continue straight ahead to reach a T-junction with South Street at the corner of a butcher shop.

WP   *At the junction there is a house opposite with a blue plaque above a house sign. Look over the road and take the last letter from the house sign.*   _____

The blue plaque is one of several in the town telling of Axminster's historical buildings. You can visit all the buildings with blue plaques on a dedicated walk – to find out more, visit the Tourist Information Centre based in the Heritage Centre.

Do not cross South Street but turn right to cross Silver Street and head down the road, which now becomes Musbury Road, keeping to the right hand pavement. The road goes downhill and when the road starts to rise again, pass a small chapel on your right. Continue up the gradual incline ignoring the turning for Widepost Lane on your right. Keep straight ahead until you see a turning opposite on your left called Boxfield Road. Cross the road carefully and head along Boxfield Road for a few yards. Look for a track on your right leading to a field. Follow this track to find your 2ⁿᵈ playground. In this area you can **Spot The Picture**.

3 From the playground, return to Boxfield Road and turn right and head up the hill, taking the first left into another road.

From the name of this road, what type of animal might you see on this hill? _____

Follow this road as it goes steeply downhill and at the bottom, look for a path on the opposite side between houses at the point where the road bends sharply to the left. This path will take you to your 3rd playground. In the playground you can **Spot The Picture**.

4 Retrace your steps using the same path between houses, and turn right at the road. After a few yards, turn right again into a road. Ignore the turning to Combe Close but take the next on the left called Purzebrook Close. Follow this road keeping on the left and a footpath will emerge in front of you. Go down this footpath and go through barriers to reach Musbury Road; this is the road you came down earlier in the walk. Cross the road carefully and turn right uphill.

Towards the top of the hill, you will see a turning left into Silver Street next to the butcher shop. Take this turning into Silver Street and then at the fork, stay right on Silver Street keeping The Axminster Inn on your left. This will lead you back to the Heritage Centre, which will be on your right.

 Rearrange the 5 **Word Puzzle** letters you have found to make a word. You may have spotted one of these on your walk.

— — — — —

14

WALK 5 – WOODBURY WAY AND OLD PARK FARM

View to Axminster from Woodbury Lane

This is a circular 3½ mile walk that starts in the town but soon takes you across fields to Woodbury Lane and Old Park Farm with good views back to Axminster and the surrounding countryside. The walk then goes through further fields before heading back to the town's Heritage Centre.

Parking: Coombe Lane Car Park, Coombefield Lane, EX13 5AX

❶ Start at the Heritage Centre which is in Silver Street (EX13 5AH). With the Centre on your left, go down Silver Street to pass the Axminster Inn on your right. Keep to the road as it bends left to meet an intersecting road. Carefully cross here and go left, following the pavement as it turns the corner into Coombefield Lane. Now continue along this lane with the car park on your left. At the top of the lane cross the road and go through the barriers to follow a path to a road just beyond an electricity substation. Turn right here and continue down the hill looking for a signposted footpath that runs along the side of the Fire Station. Here you can **Spot The Picture**.

Take the footpath and turn right before the field entrance keeping the house fences on your right. Maintain direction over two short footbridges and up the right hand side of a field ignoring the smaller stiles and paths on your right. At the top there is a junction of signposts; maintain direction straight ahead into another field that leads down to a gate and stile. Go through the gate and when you come to a footbridge over a stream, ignore the route right and go left through another gate and head up the hill with bungalows on your right. Near the top, the path forks; keep to the left and go through a gate into Woodbury Lane.

WP *Here you will find yourself next to a farm. Take the 1ˢᵗ letter from the name of the farm.* _____

Turn left and head up Woodbury Lane. There are fine views off to your left. This is a relatively quiet lane but you may encounter the occasional vehicle so take care especially near bends.

The lane continues uphill and you will come to an entrance to a driveway. Here you can **Spot The Picture**.

WP *Take the middle letter from the name of the Hall that the driveway leads to.* _____

❷ Continue up the lane for a further 200 yards until you come to a couple of houses on your right. Here you will have another opportunity to **Spot The Picture.**

Continue up the lane for a further 200 yards to the top of the hill and you will come to field access gates on your left and right. There is also a finger post showing the public footpath running across the lane. Turn left through the gate into the field. Head straight down aiming for a gate to the right of a large barn.

Go through the kissing gate and head straight across the farm courtyard through another gate into the farm's access road. Turn right and head up the access road for about 50 yards. Go through a gate on your left marked with a footpath finger post. Head up the right hand side of a field as it bends left, aiming for the top corner. At the top, go right through a gate down a narrow channel between hedges and through a further gate at the end into a field.

Go straight across this field in the direction of the telegraph pole keeping to the right of the hedgerow that bounds the opposite side of the field. At the far end, keep to the left hand edge of the field and go through a gate by a house to the road. Cross this busy road carefully, and turn right up the pavement for about 50 yards to a way-marked footpath on your left. Follow this path by going left through the kissing gate.

❸ Head down the field to the left of a large tree and aim for the gate in the hedgerow that will take you into another field. Keep to the left hand side of this field and go through the kissing gate at the bottom to emerge onto Sector Lane. Turn right here and after about 50 yards you will come to a way-marked gate in the hedge on your left. Go through this gate and follow the path over a footbridge and turn immediately left.

Maintain the same general direction avoiding the right forks as the route goes uphill across fields and through 3 farm gates. After

about ¾ of a mile, go through a gate by some houses. Go down two sets of steps and follow the pavement for a few yards. When the pavement bears right, continue across the grassy path between the stream and some houses. The path emerges onto a road by a bridge over the stream. Cross here carefully and continue straight along the road to find a footpath/cyclepath signed with a blue shared path sign. Follow this path and it will emerge onto the main road by a mini roundabout.

4 Carefully cross the road using the traffic island on your left and turn right, heading up the left hand side pavement of the road signposted for "Seaton and Honiton".

WP *Opposite the traffic island is the name of a road. Take the 1st letter from the first word and the last letter from the 2nd word.* _____

Follow this road up the hill past the Hospital across the road on your right. Shortly after passing the entrance to the Axe Valley School, you will come to the former United Reformed Church on your left.

In which year was the first chapel built on this site? _____

Continue along the road and follow it as it bends left in front of the George Hotel to a T-junction. Cross carefully and turn right to pass an NCP car park on your left. Keep to this pavement and it will lead you into Silver Street and return you to the Heritage Centre on your left.

WP Rearrange the 4 **Word Puzzle** letters you have found to make a word. You may have seen views this way on the walk.

$$\overline{} \quad \overline{} \quad \overline{} \quad \overline{}$$
1   17   4

WALK 6 – WOODLANDS, FIELDS AND FARMS

View to Hawkchurch

This is a circular 3½ mile walk on the outskirts of Axminster that will take in woodlands, fields and farms. The walk starts on a quiet lane but soon descends into woodlands and fields with expansive views to Axminster, Smallridge and Hawkchurch. The walk is mainly on woodland trails, farm tracks and through fields, some of which can be muddy in wet weather.

Parking: Roadside parking on Woodhouse Road near the junction to Beech Lane.

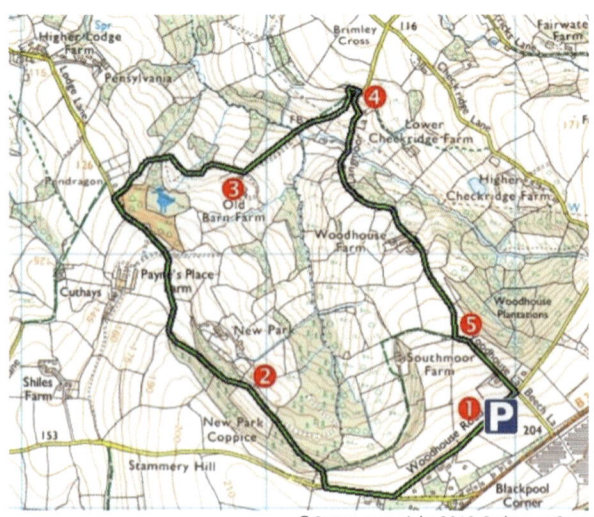

©Crown copyright 2019 Ordnance Survey. Media 052/19

From the roadside parking, head south-west along Woodhouse Road towards Axminster. A long hedge will soon appear on your right with some views to the valley if it has not become too overgrown. After 500 yards you will meet another road where you turn right.

<u>WP</u> *Take the 1ˢᵗ and last letters of the 2ⁿᵈ word written horizontally down the junction's white finger post.* _____

After a further 200 yards, look for a turning on the right, signposted as a public bridleway. Follow the track down through trees. At a finger-posted fork in the track, keep to the left hand bridleway and continue downhill. When the track bends round and down to the right next to a sign for New Park Farm, keep left along a track signed as a public bridleway.

❷ Continue uphill keeping to the track and at the top go through a metal gate that leads you into a field. Keep to the left hand side of the field. The next few fields often have cattle and can be rutted and muddy in wet weather. Views will start to open up on both sides as you make your way through a gate into another field, Continue to keep to the left hand side of the fields, and maintain direction through two further field gates as the route becomes a track and finally emerges onto a lane next to a finger post. Turn right here and follow the lane as it heads downhill and becomes a track.

Views will start to open up on your left. The track will bend right then left and there will then be a chance to **Spot The Picture.**

The track then bends to the right and you will see an old rusty vehicle in the hedgerow not far from a field gate on your left.

<u>WP</u> *Take the last two letters of the vehicle registration number.* _____

3 Go through the gate on your left into a field indicated with a blue public bridleway arrow. Head directly straight down the field to pass

another blue way-marked post on your left. Continue straight on to a footbridge, which will take you over a stream. This area can be muddy after wet weather, but the footbridge provides a good opportunity for a game of Pooh Sticks!

Cross the footbridge and pass to the left of a tree to emerge into a field. Go diagonally right, heading for the furthest far right hand corner of the field. The path here diverges slightly from the official ordnance survey map route as the direct route is too boggy to follow. There may also be a vehicle track that will also lead you to the top, so follow that if it is there.

 *You will walk under two electricity pylons – how many powerlines are there running between them?* _____

When you near the top right hand corner of the field, you will see a large gap between trees on your left. Go through the gap and turn immediately right to a gate. Go through the gate and the track will lead to a lane with a finger post on your right. Ignore the finger post pointing directly ahead and turn right down the lane.

4 The lane passes a house on your left and at the bottom of the hill it crosses a stream next to the entrance to Langmoor Farm. Take the track on the left that leads up the hill through woodland. After a few hundred yards the path levels off slightly. After a further few hundred yards, just before the path bends right, look for a sign pinned to a tree on your left.

WP *The sign asks you to keep to the path. What is the 2nd and 5th letters of the first word on the sign?* _____

Continue up the hill to an access road next to buildings. Maintain direction along the driveway to pass stables on your right. Further up the hill you will see a field of green spruce trees on your left.

At the top of the road you will reach a T-junction by the entrance to Southmoor Farm. Have a look around here to **Spot the Picture.**

5 Turn left here and follow the road as it continues uphill. The road will eventually emerge onto Woodhouse Road.

WP *Take the 2nd letter from the word written vertically on the white finger post.* _____

Turn right along Woodhouse Road to return to the parking area.

WP Rearrange the 7 **Word Puzzle** letters you have found to make a word. You may have spotted one of these on your walk.

$$\overline{}\ \overline{}\ \overline{}\ \overline{}\ \overline{}\ \overline{}\ \overline{}$$
5   8   12   9 16

WALK 7 – TRINITY HILL TO AXMINSTER

View to Axminster from Trinity Hill

This is a 'there and back again' walk of about 5 miles in total that will take you from the Nature Reserve at Trinity Hill down into the heart of Axminster. The walk starts with a short stretch along a fairly busy road without pavements, but you soon head down through the edge of woodlands with expansive views across the Axe Valley and Stockland Hill. The walk will then take you through quiet lanes and residential areas to the town's Heritage Centre, which marks the turning point for the walk. There are plenty of refreshment stops in the town if you need to rest before your return journey. See pages 37 and 38.

Parking: Off road parking area at the Trinity Hill Nature Reserve.

❶ The walk starts at one of the parking areas that provide access to the Trinity Hill Nature Reserve. This is a popular area for walking especially for dog owners and is well worth exploring.

From the parking area, facing the road, turn right and make your way along the road. This can be a busy road and there will be traffic so take extreme care along this stretch. After about 400 yards, before the road starts to bend slightly right, look for a finger-posted turning down a track on your left. Cross carefully and take this track as it leads down the side of woodlands with far reaching views across the Axe Valley and over to Stockland Hill.

❷ Follow the track as it winds downhill for almost ½ mile to a point where it levels off by a 3 point finger post next to some buildings. Ignore the finger post pointing right and keep straight ahead. Go through open gates next to a post with a yellow public footpath arrow indicating the way ahead.

The track soon starts to descend more steeply and will wind its way down to join a lane at the bottom. Keep right here and follow the lane through the tiny hamlet of Wyke past cottages on your left to a fork in the road. Take the right hand fork into Wyke Lane and follow this road as it passes

between fields. This is a quiet country lane but you might encounter the occasional car so take care, especially on the bends.

3 After about 300 yards, the lane will bend sharply left and then right taking you under a road bridge. Beyond the bridge you can **Spot The Picture.**

Continue along the lane as it passes between farm fields with views across the Axe Valley on your left. You will emerge onto a junction with a road on your right next to a white finger post.

 What is the 1ˢᵗ letter of the name written vertically on the white finger post? _____

Ignore this lane on your right and head straight on along the pavement into a residential area. Here you will start to see good views of the town and the church of St Mary's. Ignore a further road that emerges on your right.

 The road on your right takes its name from a famous Anglo-Saxon battle. What is the 5ᵗʰ letter of the first word? _____

The road then bends left at the bottom of the hill and levels off. Before you reach the main road, take a right turn into Dukes Way and follow this road up and to the right. After about 50 yards look for a path between bungalows on your left leading to a field with a children's playground. Around here you can **Spot The Picture.**

4 Go up this path and keep to the left hand side of the field aiming for the top left hand corner, where another path will take you to a road. Turn left at the road and in only a few yards you will reach the busy Musbury Road. Cross the road carefully and turn right heading towards the town. Follow this road as it passes between houses. After 150 yards, you will pass a small chapel on your left and the road will start to go uphill.

 What is the last letter of the name of this chapel? _____

After a further 150 yards at the top of the hill, you will reach the junction with Silver Street on your left next to a butcher shop. Turn left down Silver Street and then immediately right, keeping the Axminster Inn on your left. After a few further yards you will reach the Heritage Centre on your right; this marks the turning point for your walk. From here you can visit the Heritage Centre and explore the town centre.

Axminster Town Mural

 The Heritage Centre building takes its name from a famous Axminster carpet manufacturer. Take the last letter from his surname. _____

 *The Heritage Centre sits on the site of the original carpet factory. In what year was this grey building erected?* _____

To complete the walk, retrace your steps back up to the car park at Trinity Hill.

 Rearrange the 4 **Word Puzzle** letters you have found to make a word. You will have passed through this on your walk.

$$\underline{\quad} \quad \underline{\quad} \quad \underline{\quad} \quad \underline{\quad}$$
$$24 \quad\ 6 \qquad\quad 22$$

WALK 8 – THERE AND BACK ALL ABILITY AMBLE

Duck Pond

This is a level 2 mile 'there and back' route mostly on an off-road cycle path suitable for wheelchairs, mobility scooters and pushchairs. Half way along the route you can visit a duck pond.

Parking: Road side parking in North Street or any of the nearby town carparks.

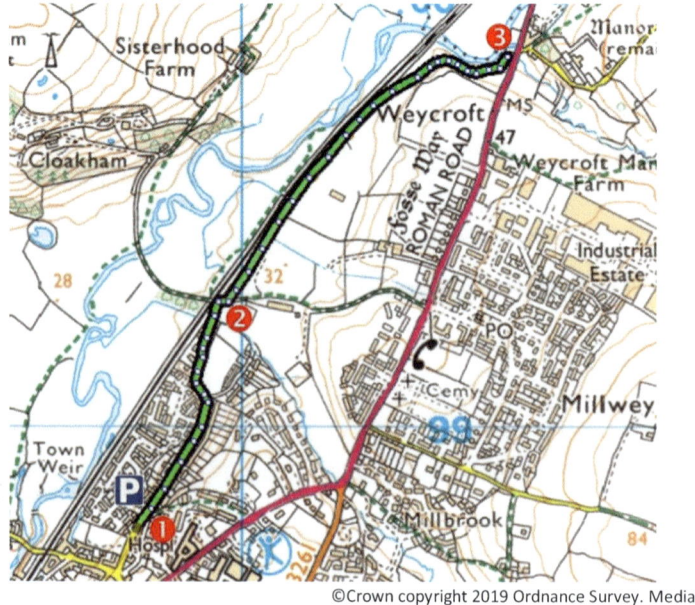

©Crown copyright 2019 Ordnance Survey. Media 052/19

❶ From North Street, with the valley views on your left, go along the right hand side pavement and continue on this road as it bends left signposted as Willhay Lane. Follow this lane to a T-junction and turn right and then immediately left through barriers to join the cycle path.

W P — *At the barriers, take the 3rd, 6th and last letter from the name on the blue finger post.* _____

❷ The cycle path now goes through a series of gates running between the railway line and the football pitches. Beyond the 2nd gate, opposite the clubhouse, you will see a duck pond on your right. The path then starts to rise slightly up to and beyond the 3rd gate and as the path bends to the right, you can **Spot The Picture.**

❸ At the end of the track you will come to a footbridge next to the Weycroft Bridge traffic lights; this marks the end of the route.

W P — *Over the footbridge there is a blue oblong sign with 3 words on it. Take both letters from the middle word.* _____

This path is part of the national cycle network – what is the number of this particular cycle route? _____

Retrace your steps and return to your starting point.

W P — Rearrange the 5 **Word Puzzle** letters you have found on your walk and make a word. This might be played near here.

— — — — —
23   18

FINAL WORD PUZZLE

Some of the **Word Puzzle** letters you have found on the walks in this book have a number against them. Fill in the letter (or letters in some cases) below corresponding to the number given. Once you have solved all the word puzzles it will reveal a final sentence.

— — — — — —
1   2   3   4   5   6

— — — — — — — —
7   8   9   10   11   12   13   14

— — — — — — —
12   15   16   7   17   18   19

— —   — — —   — — — —
3   20   4   21   22   18   23   24   20

Books in the Fun Walks series

FUN WALKING GAMES

I Spy: This classic travel game works just as well on foot. Add rules, such as "natural items only" to make it more interesting.

When You Hear ... : Select a trigger sound, such as a dog's bark or a bird's tweet. Walk in single file and when you hear the sound, the first person in the line runs to the back. Keep going until you've all had a turn.

Poetry To Go: Take turns to create your own poem. Start with a simple line like "I went for a walk with my dog" and have the others add their own rhyme in turn (eg. "and then I tripped over a log!").

Follow The Leader: Form a line and the leader makes a gesture, a sound or a funny walk. Even try walking like an animal – a crab or penguin! Everyone else has to copy the action.

Count Off: Pick something to count for the duration of the walk such as birds, dogs or cows. Make it a competition or work together as a team.

Spelling Test: Challenge each other to spell words based on what they see, such as "tree", "field" or "butterfly".

Name That Tune: Sing, hum or whistle a tune and ask your companions to guess the song and the artist or even the next lyric in the verse.

Catch: Bring a ball with you and throw it to each other as you walk. Keep count to see how long you can go before someone drops the ball.

Scavenger Hunt: Make a list of things to find such as flowers, trees, crops or unusual colours or shapes you find in nature.

Crayon Rubbing: Take some crayons and paper and do some rubbings on objects with interesting textures such as tree bark and leaves.

Bug Hunt: Look for ants, spiders and beetles and any other bugs. You might find them under logs and stones.

Leaf Collector: Collect different shaped and coloured leaves in the autumn. Take the leaves home and stick them in a scrapbook including the name of the tree they came from.

What's That Sign?: Whenever you pass a sign ask if your companions can guess what the meaning of the sign is.

Obstacle Course: Turn the walk into an obstacle course by instructing participants to touch, run around, or climb objects or jump over cracks.

Catch The Colour: Think of a colour, shout it out and watch as everyone sets off to find an object in that shade. Start with easy colours like green and yellow before moving on to rarer colours.

Shadow Tag: This is tag with a twist and is especially good at the beginning or end of the day when shadows are long. Decide who will be the chaser. The chaser catches someone by standing on the shadow of someone else; the caught person then becomes the chaser.

Leaf Catching: Played in the autumn. See how many leaves you can catch on your walk. Make it harder by using one hand.

Cloud Watching: Lie on the ground and look at the clouds passing by. Pick a cloud and ask participants to say what the cloud looks like. The winner is the one with the most imaginative answer.

Pooh Sticks: Each player throws a stick over the upstream side of a bridge into a stream or river. The winner is the person whose stick emerges first from under the bridge or a pre-agreed point downstream.

Build A Boat: If you encounter a stream or river, forage for loose material and build a raft with a sail. If it is safe to do so, place your creations into the water and have a race!

Visit the web site www.funwalks.co.uk for additional walking games.

PLACES TO VISIT IN OR NEAR AXMINSTER

Things to Do		
Archway Bookshop Church Street EX13 5AQ. 01297 33744	Axe Valley Wildlife Park Summerleaze Farm EX137RA. 01297 34472	Axminster Heritage Centre Silver Street EX13 5AH. 01297 639884
Burrow Farm Gardens Old Taunton Road Dalwood EX13 7ET. 01404 831285	Lyme Bay Winery Shute Road EX13 7PW. 01297 551355	River Cottage HQ Cookery Courses Trinity Hill Road EX13 8TB. 01297 630300
St Mary's Church Lunchtime musical recital on some Thursdays at 1pm	The Old Chapel Antiques & Craft Centre Castle Street EX13 5NP. 01297 639995	Trinity Hill Nature Reserve Trinity Hill Road EX13 5SL
Cafes and Restaurants		
Cinnamons Indian Restaurant 10 South Street EX13 5AD. 01297 631175	Costa Coffee 1 Victoria Place EX13 5NQ. 01297 35662	Far From The Madding Crowd Bar & Bistro Trinity Square EX13 5AN. 01297 598050
Furzleigh Down Farm Café with locally made ice cream. Cooks Lane EX13 5SQ. 01297 32159	Golden House Chinese restaurant 1 Lyme Street EX13 5AU. 01297 34375	Hooper's Café Castle Mount Victoria Place EX13 5NH. 01297 35821
Le Pisani Mediterranean restaurant Church Street EX13 5NX. 01297 631697	River Cottage Canteen and Deli Trinity Square EX13 5AN. 01297 631715	Safar Restaurant Indian restaurant with a lunch menu. Wood Mead Road EX13 5PJ. 01297 631607
Station Café Station Yard EX13 5PF. 01297 35221	Sublyme Contemporary Café 11 Miltons Yard EX13 5FE. 01297 631936	The Arts Café Bar Live music on Saturday's during the summer. Church Street EX13 5AQ. 01297 631455
The Community Waffle House 1 West Street EX13 5NX	The Teapot Café Millers Farm Shop Gammons Hill EX13 7RA. 01297 35290	The West Country Higgler South Street EX13 5AD. 01297 639222
Markets (every Thursday)		
Axminster Country Market Masonic Hall South Street	Axminster Market Trinity Square	

OTHER USEFUL INFORMATION

Pubs and Inns		
Axminster Inn Silver Street EX13 5AH. 01297 3494	Castle Inn Castle Hill EX13 5NN. 01297 35119	Hunter's Lodge Inn Charmouth Road EX13 5SZ. 01297 33286
Lamb Inn Lyme Road EX13 5B. 01297 33922	New Inn Kilmington EX13 7SF. 01297 33376	Red Lion Lyme Street EX13 5AU. 01297 32016
The George Hotel George Street EX13 5DW. 01297 33385	The Hind The Street, Musbury EX13 8AU. 01297 553553	The Old Inn Kilmington EX13 7RB. 01297 32096

Leisure Facilities		
Axminster Leisure Centre Lyme Road EX23 5AZ. 01297 35235	Axminister Swimming and Hydro Pool Lyme Road EX13 5AZ. 01297 35800	Cloakham Lawn and Sports Centre Chard Road EX13 5HW. 01297 34447

Takeaway		
Axe Valley Kebab House South Street EX13 5AD. 01297 631102	Lemon Plaice Fish and Chip Shop Lyme Street EX13 5AU. 01297 35888	Lucky House Chinese Takeaway Lyme Street EX13 5AU. 01297 35100

Places to Stay		
The George Hotel George Street EX13 5DW. 01297 33385	Kerrington House Musbury Road EX13 5JR. 01297 35333	Green Dragon Hotel Castle Hill EX13 5PY. 01297 647182

Parking		
EDDC Coombe Lane Coombefield Lane EX13 5AX	EDDC Poplar Mount EX13 5DZ	EDDC South Street EX13 5AD
EDDC West Street EX13 5NX	NCP Lyme Street EX13 5AT	

Transport		
Axminster Taxis 01297 34000 Paynes Premier Travel 01297 35895	Train Station Station Yard EX13 5PF	X51/X53 Buses for Lyme Regis, Charmouth and on to Dorchester & Weymouth

Public Toilets
West Street Next to Co-op Car Park. EX13 5NX